Sharks

Bull Shark

by Deborah Nuzzolo

Consulting Editor: Gail Saunders-Smith, PhD

Consultant: Jody Rake, member
Southwest Marine/Aquatic Educators' Association

Capstone press

Mankato, Minnesota

Pebble Plus is published by Capstone Press,
151 Good Counsel Drive, P.O. Box 669, Mankato, Minnesota 56002.
www.capstonepress.com

1 2 3 4 5 6 13 12 11 10 09 08

Library of Congress Cataloging-in-Publication Data
Nuzzolo, Deborah.
    Bull shark / by Deborah Nuzzolo.
    p. cm. — (Pebble plus. Sharks)
    Includes bibliographical references and index.
    Summary: "Simple text and photographs present bull sharks, their body parts,
and their behavior" — Provided by publisher.
    ISBN-13: 978-1-4296-1726-0 (hardcover)
    ISBN-10: 1-4296-1726-8 (hardcover)
    1. Bull shark — Juvenile literature. I. Title.
QL638.95.C3N89 2009
597.3'4 — dc22   2007051310

Editorial Credits
Megan Peterson, editor; Ted Williams, set designer; Kyle Grenz, book designer; Jo Miller, photo researcher

Photo Credits
Alamy/blinkwinkel, 19; David Fleetham, 20–21; Michael Patrick O'Neill, 10–11, 13, 17
Minden Pictures/Flip Nicklin, cover
Nature Picture Library/Jeff Rotman, 4–5
Peter Arnold Inc./J. Rotman Photography, 1
Seapics.com/David Kearnes, 14–15; Jeremy Stafford-Deitsch, 7
Shutterstock/Simone Conti, backgrounds
SuperStock, Inc., 9

Note to Parents and Teachers

The Sharks set supports national science standards related to the characteristics and
behavior of animals. This book describes and illustrates bull sharks. The images support
early readers in understanding the text. The repetition of words and phrases helps early
readers learn new words. This book also introduces early readers to subject-specific
vocabulary words, which are defined in the Glossary section. Early readers may need
assistance to read some words and to use the Table of Contents, Glossary, Read More,
Internet Sites, and Index sections of the book.

Table of Contents

Not Picky Eaters 4

Bull Shark Pups 8

What They Look Like 10

Hunting 16

Glossary 22

Read More 23

Internet Sites 23

Index .24

Not Picky Eaters

Bull sharks will eat
almost anything
they can catch.

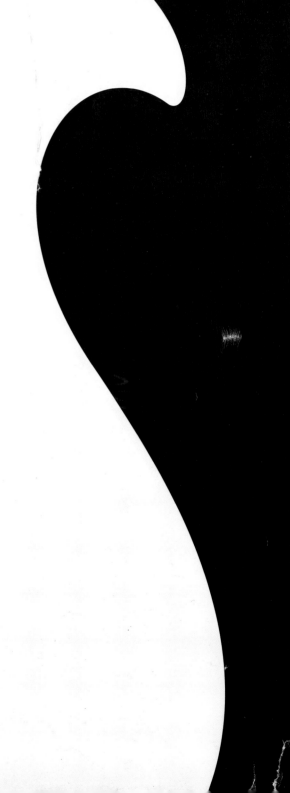

Bull sharks live in saltwater seas
and freshwater rivers.
They chase prey
in warm, shallow waters
along the shore.

Bull Shark Pups

One to 13 bull shark pups

are born at a time.

The pups are born live

and ready to hunt.

What They Look Like

Bull sharks have short, wide snouts.
Their snouts look like the nose of a bull.

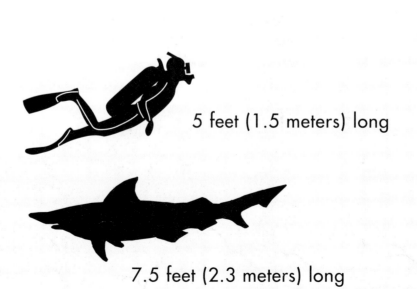

5 feet (1.5 meters) long

7.5 feet (2.3 meters) long

A bull shark's jaws
hold many sharp teeth.
The teeth have edges like saws.

A shark's skin has tiny scales called denticles.
These scales make shark skin feel like sandpaper.

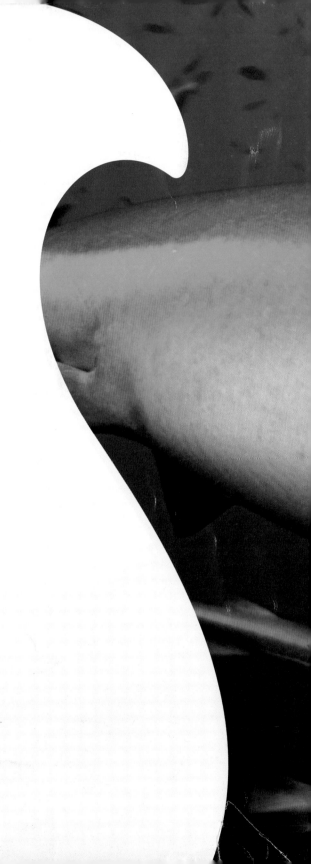

Hunting

Bull sharks hunt fish, dolphins, sea turtles, and other sharks.

Bull sharks can hear very well.

They listen for prey.

19

When a bull shark finds prey,
it moves fast.
This fierce fish was born to hunt.

Glossary

denticles — small, toothlike scales that cover a shark's skin

fierce — violent or dangerous

freshwater — water that does not have salt; most ponds, rivers, lakes, and streams are freshwater; oceans are saltwater.

prey — an animal hunted by another animal for food

pup — a young shark

shallow — not deep

shore — the place where the water meets land; many sharks swim in the shallow water near the shore.

snout — the front part of a shark's head that includes the nose, mouth, and jaws

Read More

Crossingham, John, and Bobbie Kalman. *The Life Cycle of a Shark.* The Life Cycle Series. New York: Crabtree, 2006.

Lindeen, Carol K. *Sharks.* Under the Sea. Mankato, Minn.: Capstone Press, 2005.

Simon, Seymour. *Sharks.* New York: Collins, 2006.

Internet Sites

FactHound offers a safe, fun way to find Internet sites related to this book. All of the sites on FactHound have been researched by our staff.

Here's how:

1. Visit *www.facthound.com*

2. Choose your grade level.

3. Type in this book ID **1429617268** for age-appropriate sites. You may also browse subjects by clicking on letters, or by clicking on pictures and words.

4. Click on the **Fetch It** button.

FactHound will fetch the best sites for you!

Index

birth, 8

body parts, 10, 12, 14

denticles, 14

fish, 16, 20

freshwater, 6

habitat, 6

hearing, 18

hunting, 4, 6, 8, 16,
    18, 20

jaws, 12

prey, 6, 16, 18, 20

pups, 8

saltwater, 6

size, 10

skin, 14

snouts, 10

teeth, 12

Word Count: 129
Grade: 1
Early-Intervention Level: 18